A Teacher's Guide to
A Walk In the Rainforest

Lesson plans for the book
A Walk in the Rainforest, by Kristin Joy Pratt

by Bruce & Carol Malnor

Bruce and Carol Malnor together have over 40 years of educational experience. Bruce has been a classroom teacher, elementary school principal, and is a Brain Gym instructor. Carol has taught elementary, junior high and high school, and has helped found two alternative high schools. They are directors of the Education for Life Foundation and have conducted workshops for educators throughout the U.S., as well as in Canada, Germany and Italy.

Bruce and Carol share a lifelong appreciation of nature. They enjoy taking a walk through a rainforest whenever they have the opportunity.

Sharing Nature with Children Series

Dedication

To our parents and all of the teachers
who have helped and inspired us.

And to all those who help children to walk in beauty.

NO MATTER HOW SHORT, NO MATTER HOW LONG,
NO MATTER HOW BIG, HOW SMART OR HOW STRONG,
ALL LIFE HAS A PLACE, A PURPOSE AND WORTH.
ALL LIFE IS IMPORTANT ON OUR PLANET EARTH.
—BRM & CLM

Publisher's Cataloguing-in-Publication
(Provided by Quality Books, Inc.)

Malnor, Bruce.
  Teacher's guide to A walk in the rainforest / by Bruce and Carol Malnor.
  p. cm. — (Sharing Nature with Children series)
  Includes bibliographical references.
  ISBN: 1-883220-74-2

  1. Pratt, Kristin Joy. Walk in the rainforest. 2. Rain forests—Study and teaching (Elementary)—Activity programs. 3. Ecology—Study and teaching (elementary)—Activity programs. 4. Teaching—Aids and devices. I. Malnor, Carol. II. Pratt, Kristin Joy. Walk in the rainforest. III. Title.

QH541.5.R27M35 1998   577.34'071
                                       QBI98-234

Published by DAWN Publications
12402 Bitney Springs Road
Nevada City, CA 95959
e-mail: nature@DawnPub.com
website: www.DawnPub.com

Printed in Canada
10 9 8 7 6 5 4 3 2
First Edition

Illustrations by Kristin Joy Pratt and Sarah Brink
Computer production by Rob Froelick and Renee Glenn
Designed by Lee Ann Brook

Table of Contents

Dear Teacher,

Just as the rainforest ecosystem is only as vital as the health of its individual parts, a society is only as strong as the character development of each of its members. As a teacher you know how powerfully the character of each student can affect the whole class. This teacher's guide is designed to build character while it teaches about the rainforest environment. Using the engaging book *A Walk in the Rainforest* by Kristin Joy Pratt as a springboard, this guide presents eighteen lesson plans plus additional extension activities that teach character qualities as well as core science and language arts concepts.

Teaching children to be sensitive and responsible to the environment involves much more than just teaching them about the water cycle or the food web. Research has found that students actually respond negatively to the environment if they are only taught facts about the environment, what is wrong with it, and what they need to do to fix it. *Sharing Nature With Children Teacher's Guides* focus on helping students develop the skills, qualities, and character traits that allow them to relate to others and the environment in positive, healthy ways. Life skills such as respect, responsibility, and cooperation extend far beyond the school setting; they can be applied to the rainforest as well as the ocean, to the family as well as the classroom. The rainforest animals in *A Walk in the Rainforest* provide a meaningful curriculum into which important life skills can be incorporated.

The lesson plans are most suitable for grades 3 to 6, but can be adapted for some 7th or even 8th grade classes. Unless otherwise stated, the lessons can be completed in a 45 to 60 minute class period; a few may need additional time. This time can be adjusted by including more or less student discussion and sharing. For teachers who use block scheduling, many lessons can be combined or used back to back creating a full 90 to 120 minute class session.

Each lesson includes the following elements, which in our experience provide the greatest possible educational impact: *Flow Learning™ Format; Tools of Maturity; Benchmarks; Skills for Living; Mind Mapping; and Brain Compatible Activities.* These components are explained more fully on the following pages.

Wishing you and your students a joyful walk together toward greater growth and understanding.

Bruce and Carol Malnor

The Whys and Hows

Flow Learning™

Why: "Give me a lever long enough and a place to stand and I can move the world." When Archimedes said this, he was emphasizing the power of the lever. Simple tools can be some of the most effective. Flow Learning™ is one such tool for us as educators. It was developed by Joseph Cornell, the famous nature educator and author of *Sharing Nature With Children*. We use Flow Learning™ because it is based on how people learn. The Flow Learning™ process captures students' interest in the lesson right from the beginning, thus eliminating or minimizing many discipline problems. It's a simple, effective way to uplift a group's energy. There are four steps in Flow Learning™:

1. Awaken Enthusiasm—Children learn if the subject matter is meaningful, useful, fun, or in some way engages their emotions. Time spent in creating an atmosphere of curiosity, amusement, or personal interest is invaluable because once students' enthusiasm is engaged, their energy can be focused on the upcoming lesson.

2. Focus Attention—Some students' minds can be compared to a team of wild horses running out of control. Without concentration no true learning can take place. The power of a laser beam lies in its intense focus; so it is with our thoughts. This guide uses the beautiful illustrations and interesting plants and animals in *A Walk in the Rainforest*, by Kristin Joy Pratt to focus attention and increase learning capacity.

3. Direct Experience—Once students' interest and energy is awakened and focused, the stage is set for a direct experience. Each lesson plan is designed to provide an experience that expands the students' knowledge base, provides an opportunity to use the information to create or synthesize something new, or inspires new awareness.

4. Share Inspiration—Each lesson provides an interesting way for students to reflect together on what they have learned. In our fast-paced world, students and teachers alike often rush from one activity to another. Yet taking the time to reflect upon an experience can strengthen and deepen that experience. It need not take long. It can be as simple as responding to a few questions, writing a journal entry, or drawing a picture. Goethe said, "A joy shared is a joy doubled." Giving students the opportunity to share their experience increases the learning for the entire class.

How: You can experience and understand the Flow Learning™ process by simply following the lesson plans. As its name suggests, Flow Learning™ is flexible, so feel free to make adjustments in the lessons. Some classes may need greater emphasis given to Awaken Enthusiasm activities while others may need more time for Focus Attention. Shorten or lengthen these parts of the lesson to suit your students' specific needs. The Direct Experience meets the stated objective of the lesson; choose activities according to what you want your students to learn or experience.

Benchmarks

Why: Maintaining high standards in the classroom aids student achievement. The benchmarks in *Content Knowledge: A Compendium of Standards and Benchmarks for K-12 Education*, by John S. Kendall and Robert J. Marzano, identify the skills and knowledge which are essential for all students.

How: Each lesson plan in this guide identifies one or more benchmarks which primarily relate to Science, Life Skills or Language Arts. Choose activities which will meet the standards your students are working towards.

Skills for Living

Why: One of our goals as teachers is to help our students lead successful lives. True success is measured not by material standards, but by quality of life: happiness, fulfillment, joy. The attitudes and qualities which lead us toward true success are called Skills for Living. Like any skill, they can be taught and practiced. Students' character development affects not only them, but also the future of our country and our planet.

How: Each lesson focuses on one or more of the Skills for Living. Simply doing the activities gives students practice with the skill. It can also be helpful for students to have these skills identified by name so that they can understand the skill more completely and apply it in other contexts. With continued practice and application, students internalize the Skills for Living and make them their own. A list of Skills for Living can be found on page 47.

Tools of Maturity

Why: One goal of education is to encourage students to expand their awareness to include the realities of every living thing. We define maturity as the ability to relate to others' realities. Greater and greater maturity (expansion of awareness) leads to greater and greater success and happiness in life. Just as carpenters have many tools which they use to build a house, as human beings we all have been given "tools" to use which lead us toward greater expansion. These "tools of maturity" are the body, the mind (intellect), our feelings, and our will power. Each tool has a specific goal: *body*—physical vitality and energy control; *intellect*—the ability to think clearly and practically; *feelings*—emotional calmness and sensitivity; *will power*—dynamic persistence to set and accomplish goals. Students usually have a natural preference for one or two of the tools. Their preference indicates the areas in which they feel most capable and confident. As they develop all four tools of maturity in a balanced, harmonious way, they will learn to explore their full potential.

How: Each lesson plan focuses on the development of one or more of these tools. The tools indicated in the lesson heading relate to the Direct Experience part of the lesson. Choosing lessons according to the Tools of Maturity is just another way to insure that the strengths, abilities, and needs of all students are being addressed. Some lessons incorporate all four tools, while others give students a choice of activities and therefore a choice as to which tool they will use. There are many ways to incorporate the tools of maturity into all of your lessons. A list of simple suggestions can be found on page 47.

Mind Mapping

Why: Graphic organizers have many different names: story webs, semantic maps, concept maps, and mind maps. We use the term "Mind Map." Mind Maps are visible representations of information using either pictures, words, or a combination of both. Through Mind Mapping students develop organizational skills as well as thinking skills—both the sequential and gestalt (left and right) hemispheres of the brain are used. Comprehension and memory increase as students Mind Map information they read or hear.

How: The Mind Maps in this Teacher's Guide can be used in a variety of ways:

- To introduce an animal
- To focus students' attention before doing other activities
- To review information either from memory or from the text
- To be completed as a homework assignment
- To be done by individual students or as a small group activity
- To include words, pictures, or a combination of both

The activity entitled "Water—Mind Mapping Made Easy" on page 8 introduces the concept of mind mapping to students. Mind Maps are included for each of the rainforest animals for which there are lesson plans. They are meant to serve only as guides; there is not just one "right" way to make a Mind Map. Research shows that Mind Maps are much more effective and useful when students create them adding their own perspective and individuality.

Brainstorming, Discussions, and Sharing

Why: Brainstorming, discussions, and sharing are a part of every lesson, with different student groupings focusing on different outcomes:

- With a partner—Students sharing one-on-one gives everyone a chance to talk without taking a lot of class time.
- In a small group—Collaboration stimulates creative thinking.
- By individual students presented to the whole class—Students have opportunities to practice poise in front of a group.
- Privately through a journal entry—Non-verbal activities balance the usual outward way of sharing with a more introspective approach.

We encourage you to experiment with different types of student groupings to suit the particular dynamics of your class. Variety helps to keep student responses fresh and enthusiastic.

How: It is essential to establish an environment in which students can share without fear of ridicule. Before beginning any brainstorming activity, review the guidelines for brainstorming with students: (1) Every response is acceptable; tell students not to be concerned with accuracy at this point in the lesson. (2) Encourage lots of variety and unique responses; remind students that the "craziest" response often leads to the best idea. (3) Absolutely no put downs are allowed; have clear consequences for any student who uses a put down.

The conclusion of a lesson is the time to acknowledge and celebrate student learning. Teach students to share their thoughts and feelings by (1) sharing your own thoughts and feelings, (2) giving heart-felt appreciative comments to students, (3) asking reflective questions, (4) encouraging all students to participate, (5) waiting patiently for students to collect their thoughts before speaking; a minute of silence can seem like a very long time, but research shows student responses are more complex and complete when there is adequate wait time.

Brain-Compatible Teaching

Why: In the last ten years research has greatly expanded our understanding of how the brain functions. The activities in this guide are brain-compatible (a term coined by Leslie Hart in *Human Brain and Human Learning*) because they incorporate strategies which make learning easier.

How: The activities in this guide are brain-compatible because they:
- *Encourage collaboration between students.* The exchange of ideas fosters divergent thinking and creativity.
- *Engage students' feelings along with their intellect.* Research shows that learning and memory are enhanced when students have an emotional connection with the subject matter—the head and heart working together.
- *Connect the information to real life experiences.* Learning becomes meaningful when students make connections and use the information immediately in their own lives.
- *Co-create a rich learning environment.* When students contribute to creating visual displays, they are given the messages, "Your work is valuable," "What you do matters," or "This is important to others." Increased self-esteem results in greater risk-taking and participation, thus increasing learning.

Home and Habitat

Why: The three different environments (ocean, rainforest, and sky) described by Kristin Pratt's three books are really three different *homes*. As Daphne the Damselfly said in *A Fly in the Sky*, "She discovered this space was more than a place; it was her home." Home is where we feel most comfortable, where we are nourished and nurtured, where we live day-to-day. Each of the homes Kristin writes about is unique and each one is essential for the health and well-being of our larger home: the Earth.

How: In *A Walk in the Rainforest,* XYZ the ant goes exploring in the rainforest. Like XYZ, the best way for students to really understand the rainforest is to have a direct experience of it; in lieu of an actual trip to the rainforest, visit a botanical garden, museum, zoo, or even a pet store. For specific ideas about how to turn your classroom into a rainforest see "Water—Creating a Rainforest Environment" on page 10.

Water

Mind Mapping
Made Easy

Objectives	• Introduce and practice Mind Mapping • Introduce the topic of rainforest plants and animals
Tools of Maturity	• Intellect
Benchmarks	• Identifies information-organizing strategies that are personally most useful (Language Arts 7, Level III)
Skills for Living	• Orderliness
Materials	• Copy of Water Mind Map—1 per student; colored pencils or crayons

Awaken Enthusiasm

Ask the class to brainstorm the different plants and animals that they think can be found in the rainforest. Review the guidelines of brainstorming with students. Allow three minutes. If done in small groups, have each group share three of their responses with the rest of the class.

Focus Attention

Beginning with the letter "A", say the letters of the alphabet one at a time. Pause after each letter allowing students time to share the names of any plants or animals they listed that begin with that letter. Did every letter have a plant or animal?

Direct Experience

Show students the book *A Walk in the Rainforest* and tell them that they are going to learn about rainforest inhabitants A through Z. Pass out copies of the Water Mind Map and explain that they should listen carefully while you read about the water, the most essential part of the rainforest environment. As they hear the information that appears on the Mind Map, they should use their colored pencils to color in the appropriate circles. Read aloud about water, pausing briefly after each sentence.

Share Inspiration

Ask the students how the information was organized on the Mind Map. (It begins at the center with the name "water" and moves outward. Each group of connected circles is about the same topic.) All Mind Maps begin with a central theme and add details. Explain to the students that Mind Maps are an excellent way to organize information. Often times the more colorful and creative a Mind Map is, the easier it is to remember the information on it. Mind Mapping is a more visual way of showing the same information that is contained in an outline.

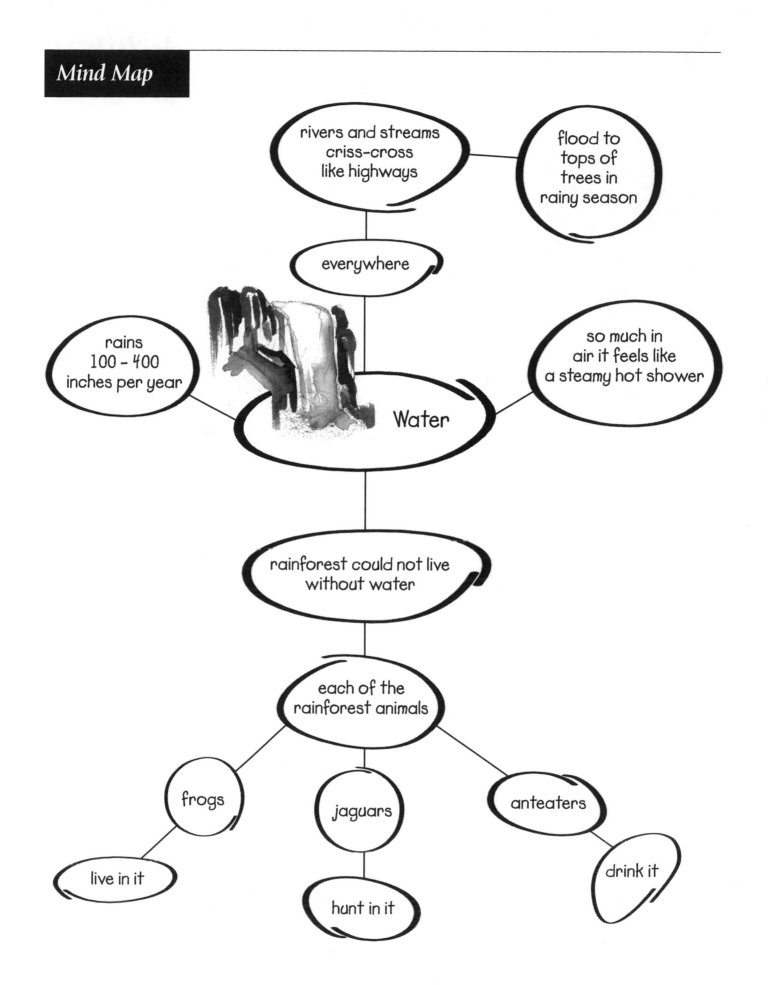

rivers and streams criss-cross like highways

flood to tops of trees in rainy season

everywhere

rains 100 – 400 inches per year

Water

so much in air it feels like a steamy hot shower

rainforest could not live without water

each of the rainforest animals

frogs

jaguars

anteaters

live in it

hunt in it

drink it

Water  Creating a Rainforest Environment

Objectives	• Learn the characteristics of a rainforest • Simulate a rainforest environment
Tools of Maturity	• Intellect, body
Benchmarks	• Understands the characteristics of ecosystems on Earth's surface (Geography 8, Level II and III); makes decisions based on data obtained and the criteria identified, takes action to implement the decision (Life Skills: Thinking and Reasoning 6, Level III)
Skills for Living	• Creativity, cooperation
Materials	• Rainforest Characteristics (Copy Master, page 12); various art supplies and craft materials determined by student ideas • Time: This activity can take from two days up to six weeks.

Awaken Enthusiasm

Divide the class into small groups. Ask the groups to brainstorm the characteristics of a rainforest.

Focus Attention

Give each group a copy of the Rainforest Characteristics handout. Have them put a check next to any of the characteristics that they brainstormed. If they came up with responses that are not on the handout, have them check with you for accuracy.

Direct Experience

Tell the students that they are going to create a rainforest in the classroom that includes all of the characteristics on their handout. Have them brainstorm ways to simulate the characteristics using common arts and crafts supplies and materials. Tell students to write their ideas on the Rainforest Characteristic handout. Give them additional criteria to follow such as time allowed to complete the project, amount of space they can use in the classroom, cost of supplies, etc. Encourage students to use their imaginations. Offer ideas and suggestions if they need help getting started. The following list gives ideas that have been tried in other classrooms:

rainfall: 1) make a fountain using a small submersible pump in a container filled with rocks, 2) make drops of water from shiny, iridescent paper and hang from the ceiling

hot: turn up the thermostat

humid: bring in a humidifier

water everywhere: 1) use a kiddie wading pool and fill it with water, 2) lay blue plastic (from inexpensive tablecloths) on the floor

exists around the world at the equator: string a red ribbon around the center of the room

biodiversity: 1) bring in pets such as birds, frogs, iguanas: 2) bring in stuffed animals: 3) make masks or models of animals: 4) put up posters of rainforest life

layered vegetation: 1) set up ladders and place plants on the rungs: 2) each student brings in one plant: 3) make terrariums: 4) stack tables and desks on top of each other: 5) build simple perches: 6) dye sheets green and use tempera paint to paint a backdrop

forest canopy: hang green overlapping sheets across the top of the ceiling

dim forest floor: 1) paint windows green with tempera paint (mixing paint with a little dish soap makes cleanup easier): 2) replace regular light bulbs with green colored light bulbs

leaves with drip tips: make leaves out of construction paper

colorful flowers: use colored tissue paper

vines: use rope or rolled brown paper bags

trees with buttress roots: stack 3 garbage cans on top of each other and wrap with corrugated cardboard, use papier mache to attach roots along the sides

epiphytes: attach plants and flowers to the trees

lots of insects: 1) bring in plastic bugs: 2) make or buy an ant farm

sounds: bring in a rainforest sounds tape

Share Inspiration

Have small groups present their ideas and, as a class, use the criteria to select the ideas that can work. Take several days to create the environment. This project can be done in stages as the class learns about the plants and animals in greater depth. As a culminating project, hold a Rainforest Open House and serve rainforest treats (foods made from rainforest products) such as **banana** splits made with **vanilla** ice cream and **chocolate** sauce topped with **nuts**.

Rainforest Characteristics

Rainfall—80 inches minimum annually; 200 inches in many rainforests, 400 inches in a few places

Hot temperatures—between 70 and 85 degrees Fahrenheit with little variation between daytime highs and nighttime lows

Humid—70% humidity during the day, 95% at night

Water everywhere—rivers and streams criss-cross the landscape

Circle the earth for 20 degrees of latitude on either side of the equator

Biodiversity—more than half of all the species of plants and animals in the world make their home there

Layered vegetation—emergent trees, canopy layer, understory, and forest floor

Lots of insects

Leaves have drip tips

Many epiphytes

Trees have buttress roots—the layer of soil is shallow and poor in nutrients

Copy Master

Water

The Water Cycle and Interdependence

Objectives	• Learn the water cycle • Pantomime the interdependence in the rainforest ecosystem
Tools of Maturity	• Body
Benchmarks	• Understands how species depend on one another and on the environment for survival (Science 7, Levels I-III); understands the function and dynamics of ecosystems, knows plants and animals associated with various vegetation and climate regions (Geography 8, Levels II and III); uses acting skills (The Arts: Theater 2, Levels II and III)
Skills for Living	• Creativity, cooperation
Materials	• (Optional) student masks or costumes and sound effects

Awaken Enthusiasm

Pantomime various rainforest creatures and have students guess their identity. End by pantomiming rain falling.

Focus Attention

Have students mimic you as you pantomime the water cycle (precipitation, evaporation, condensation). Begin again with rain falling, flowing into tiny streams and bigger rivers, the sun shining, water evaporating into the air, clouds forming, a huge storm developing with lots of wind and rain, a flood raging, the waters receding, and a gentle rain falling.

Direct Experience

Review the elements of the water cycle with the students. Refer to the Mind Map information about water, emphasizing that all the plants and animals of the rainforest depend on water. Have students choose one of the plants or animals from *A Walk in the Rainforest* to pantomime. Also include elements from the water cycle. Encourage students to be expressive and creative with their body movements, facial expressions, and sound effects. (Optional: supply art materials and/or face paint to create costumes.) Begin the pantomime with the water elements and add the plants and animals one at a time until the entire class is involved in the rainforest scene.

Share Inspiration

Tell each character to describe how he is dependent upon water; students can refer to the information about their character in *A Walk in the Rainforest*. Point out the interdependence between species and the environment. Have students notice who they depend on and who depends upon them; for example, the bromeliad depends upon the tree and the frog depends upon the bromeliad and all three depend upon water.

Dragonfly

Objectives	• Practice Mind Mapping information and cooperative learning • Play an active game that reviews information
Tools of Maturity	• Body, intellect
Benchmarks	• Knows that plants and animals have life cycles which include birth, growth, and development, reproduction, and death; knows that plants and animals have a great variety of body plans and internal structures that contribute to their being able to make or find food and reproduce (Science 4, Levels II and III); understands the social and personal responsibility associated with participation in physical activity (Physical Education 4, Levels II and III)
Skills for Living	• Cooperation
Materials	• Dragonfly Fact Cards (Copy Master, page 15), copied and cut up—1 fact per student; white paper (approximately 24 inches square)—one sheet per student group; colorful markers; soft rubber ball; large playing area • Time: Allow two class sessions for this activity, one to prepare Mind Maps and one to play the game.

Awaken Enthusiasm

At the beginning of class, have students pick a Dragonfly Fact Card. Tell students to form a five-person group with four others without talking; each person in the group should have a different fact card. All groups should have fact cards about a dragonfly's wings, body, eyes, habitat, and eating.

Focus Attention

Working cooperatively, using a large sheet of white paper, have students combine their information on one Mind Map. Tell them to use the "4 C's" in making their mind maps: Complete, Clear, Colorful, and Creative. When finished, instruct students to teach each other all of the dragonfly information which will be important for them to know in playing a game the next day.

Direct Experience

Remind students that dragonflies catch their food in midair. The object of the game is to catch a ball in midair and tag another student. Designate age-appropriate boundaries. Choose one player to be the "dragonfly" and stand in the middle of the playing area; other students stand within a five foot radius around the "dragonfly." The dragonfly throws the rubber ball high into the air, simultaneously calling out the name of one of the other students. The student whose name is called catches the ball and yells "freeze!" All runners stop. The student who caught the ball takes up to three giant steps in any direction and throws the ball trying to hit another student. If a student is hit with the ball, he has ten seconds to state a dragonfly fact. If he cannot state a fact or states one incorrectly, he becomes the dragonfly and a new round begins. If he correctly states a fact, a new round of the game begins with the original dragonfly throwing the ball. No facts can be repeated during the course of the game, making it progressively harder for players to remain free. If no one is hit by the thrown ball the dragonfly remains the thrower and a new round begins.

Share Inspiration

Post completed Mind Maps around the room. Have students notice similarities and differences. Ask them to share appreciative comments for members in their group. Discuss playing the game. Ask them if making the Mind Maps helped them to remember the information. What group skills were involved in playing the game? (E.g. physical speed, accurate throwing, memory, following the rules.) Discuss any variations they can think of to apply the game to other learning tasks.

Dragonfly Fact Cards

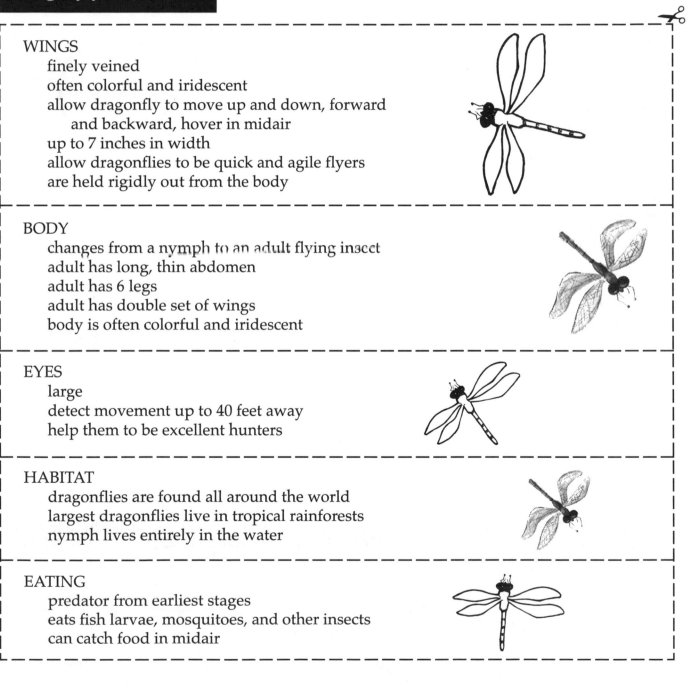

WINGS
   finely veined
   often colorful and iridescent
   allow dragonfly to move up and down, forward
      and backward, hover in midair
   up to 7 inches in width
   allow dragonflies to be quick and agile flyers
   are held rigidly out from the body

BODY
   changes from a nymph to an adult flying insect
   adult has long, thin abdomen
   adult has 6 legs
   adult has double set of wings
   body is often colorful and iridescent

EYES
   large
   detect movement up to 40 feet away
   help them to be excellent hunters

HABITAT
   dragonflies are found all around the world
   largest dragonflies live in tropical rainforests
   nymph lives entirely in the water

EATING
   predator from earliest stages
   eats fish larvae, mosquitoes, and other insects
   can catch food in midair

Copy Master for cut out

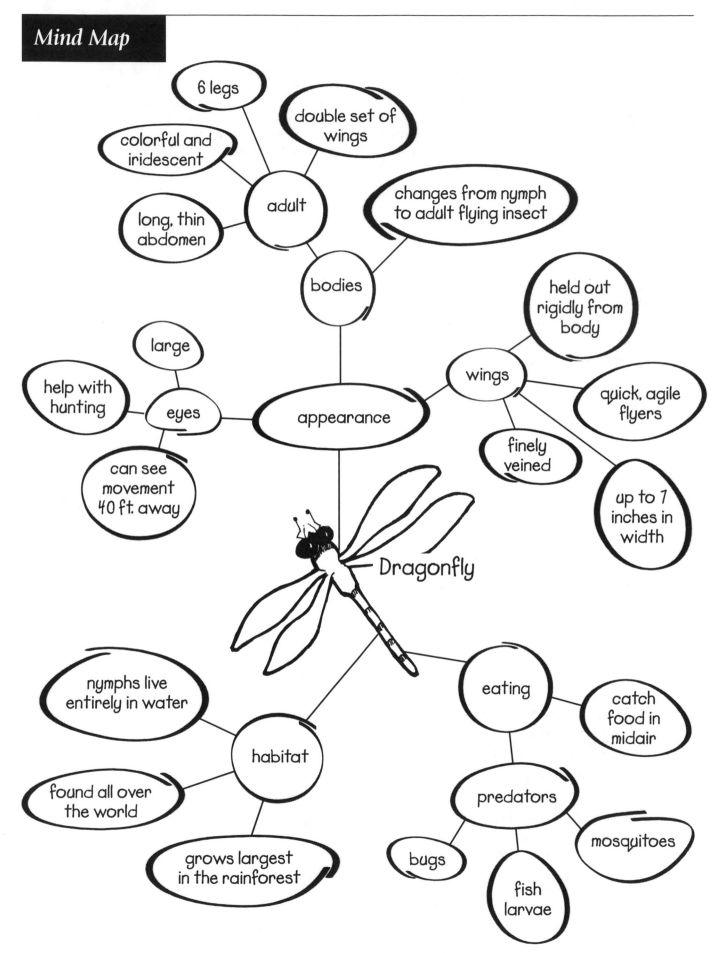

6 legs

double set of wings

colorful and iridescent

long, thin abdomen

adult

changes from nymph to adult flying insect

bodies

held out rigidly from body

large

help with hunting

eyes

appearance

wings

quick, agile flyers

can see movement 40 ft. away

finely veined

up to 7 inches in width

Dragonfly

nymphs live entirely in water

habitat

eating

catch food in midair

found all over the world

predators

grows largest in the rainforest

bugs

mosquitoes

fish larvae

Gorilla

Mirror Mime Time

Objectives	• Imitate a partner's movements • Become aware of body language and its connection to emotions • Make careful observations
Tools of Maturity	• Body
Benchmarks	• Uses a variety of basic and advanced movement forms (Physical Education 1, Level I); uses nonverbal communication effectively (Life Skills: Working with Others 4, Level IV); knows that learning can come from careful observations and simple experiments and that scientists develop explanations using observations and what they already know about the world (Science 15, Levels I and II)
Skills for Living	• Cooperation, sensitivity
Materials	• Classical music tape

Awaken Enthusiasm

Tell the class that George Schaller and Dian Fossey, two important researchers into gorilla behavior, discovered that by imitating gorilla behavior they were able to gain the gorillas' confidence and get very close to them. Ask students to imitate your movements. Assume various positions that would be interesting and somewhat challenging for your students to copy such as standing on one foot, touching your toes, doing ten jumping jacks.

Focus Attention

Instruct each student to think of a simple movement. One at a time have a student perform his or her movement and have the rest of the class imitate it. You can also suggest that they add a sound (but no words) to accompany the movement. Proceed around the class until every one has had a turn.

Direct Experience

Pair students and have them stand opposite each other about one foot apart. Designate one student as the "mover" and the other as the "mirror." The mover slowly moves his arms, legs, and body while the mirror duplicates the mover's movements exactly as if being a mirror image. Playing classical music in the background encourages smooth, fluid movements. After a minute or two, have the partners switch roles. Next have students become "changing mirrors." They should take turns being the mover and mirror without verbally communicating, just silently changing roles and being sensitive to each other. Practice changing mirrors for 1-2 minutes.

Share Inspiration

When finished discuss, with each other which role was easier, being the mover or the mirror. Ask students how they changed their vision to watch the whole body of their partner. (They needed to use peripheral vision.) What kinds of movements did they especially enjoy? Not enjoy? How difficult was it for them to play changing mirrors? Could they tune into the other person without talking?

Extension: The following two extension activities closely relate to movement and observation.

17

A Closer Look: Schaller and Fosey learned about gorillas through careful observation; it took time and patience. Have students carefully watch an animal over a several day period. They can choose a pet in their home or an animal they regularly see outside such as a squirrel, bird, or horse. Have them write down observations they make in one or more of these categories: eating, sleeping, grooming, moving about, interacting with other animals, interacting with humans. Ask students to draw conclusions about the animal's life based upon their observations. What limitations are they faced with in drawing their conclusions? Do they think scientists face these same kinds of limitations? How can they be overcome? For older students, this could be a good time to explain the nature of scientific inquiry and the scientific method.

Emotion Charades: Explain that gorillas use body language to express emotion and so do humans. Write various emotions on slips of paper. One at a time, have each student draw a slip and act out the emotion using facial expressions and body language. Students can also form small groups and perform a skit incorporating all of the emotions.

Mind Map

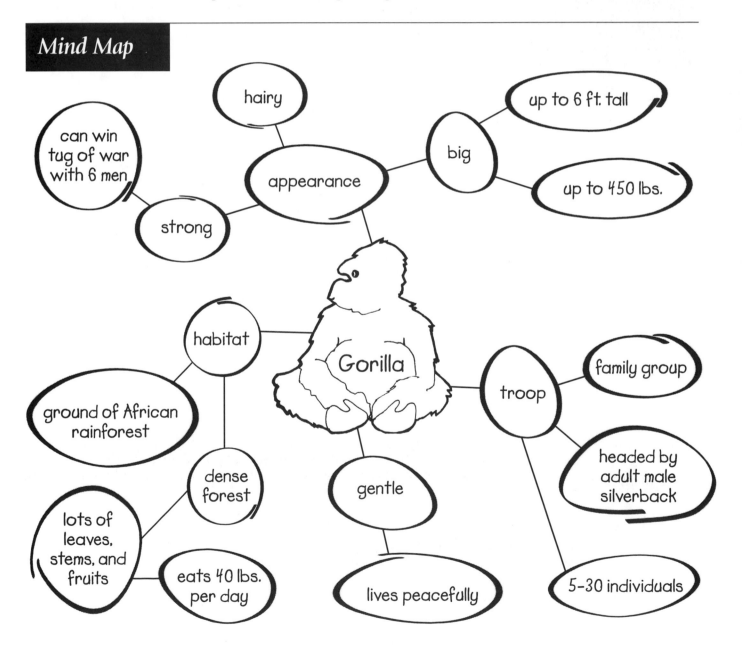

Jaguar  Rituals, Traditions, and Ceremonies

Objectives	• Plan and carry out a class ritual
Tools of Maturity	• Feeling
Benchmarks	• Understands that each culture has distinctive patterns of behavior that are usually practiced by most of the people who grow up in it (Behavioral Studies 1, Level III); contributes to the overall effort of a group (Life Skills 1, Level IV)
Skills for Living	• Respect, sensitivity
Materials	• Ritual Questions (Copy Master, page 20)—1 per group • Time: Allow one class period to plan the ritual and others to carry it out.

Awaken Enthusiasm

Ask students to share how they celebrate their family birthdays. As students share, take time to notice some of the similarities and differences.

Focus Attention

Explain to the class that a birthday celebration is a ritual: a ceremony that is performed to honor a special person, time, event, or circumstance. Ask students to identify other rituals (e.g., wedding ceremony, funeral, baptism, communion, graduation, bar or bas mitzvah). In Central America the jaguar plays an important role in a religious ritual because it is considered a very special and sacred animal. Examples of other sacred animals include the crane (Japan), the white buffalo and the eagle (Native American), the polar bear (Eskimo), and the cow (India). Tell the class that they will choose an animal and develop their own ritual.

Direct Experience

Divide the class into groups of three to five students each. Instruct them to answer the questions on the following page.

Share Inspiration

Have student groups share their ideas. As a class decide which rituals your class can actually perform during the school year. Plan a specific time to conduct your rituals and involve students in the planning and implementing processes.

Ritual Questions

What will you celebrate? What special school event do you want to remember with a ritual?

What animal will you include in your ritual? Why is this animal the best one to use? How will you use it?

Who do you want to attend the ritual? Parents, brothers or sisters, friends, principal? Will they have a part to play or will they be observers?

Where will your ritual take place? Inside or outside? Giving the site a special cleaning is often a part of ritual preparations. Do you want to decorate the site in any way?

When will your ritual take place? Could your class arrange to do the ritual after school or in the evening? Is there a particular season that is most appropriate for your ritual? How long will your ritual last?

How will you celebrate? What will you do? Traditional elements of ritual include food, dress, music, and some type of activity.

Copy Master

20

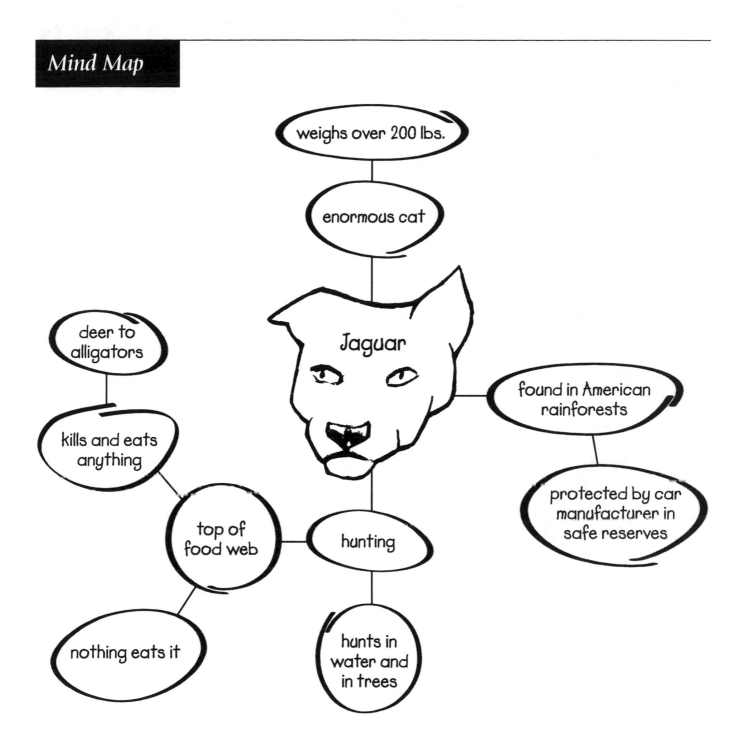

Jaguar  *Special Spots*

Objectives	• Research a topic • Give an oral presentation • Complete a chart and compare similarities and differences
Tools of Maturity	• Intellect
Benchmarks	• Understands how species depend on one another and on the environment for survival (Science 7, Levels II and III); effectively gathers and uses information for research purposes (Language Arts 4, Levels II and III); effectively uses mental processes that are based on identifying similarities and differences; compares, contrasts, and classifies (Life Skills: Thinking 3, Levels II and III); contributes to the overall effort of the group (Life Skills: Working with Others 1, Level IV)
Skills for Living	• Cooperation, appreciation
Materials	• Age appropriate books and materials with information about the jaguar, ocelot, cheetah, leopard, snow leopard, and tiger; an equal number of Spot Squares (Copy Master, page 23)—1 per student; Information Chart (Copy Master, page 45)—1 per student group • Preparation: Tape one Spot Square under each student chair • Time: One class needed for preparing the report and one for report presentations.

Awaken Enthusiasm

When it is time for class to begin, have students reach under their chairs and remove the Spot Squares you've taped there. Instruct them to find the others in class who have exactly the same type of spot. Students with the same type of spots form a cooperative learning group.

Focus Attention

Ask students if they can identify the animal with their type of spot. Give them the correct answer and tell them that they will have time to research their animal, fill in a chart with the information, and report what they have learned to the rest of the class. Have each group member choose one of the following topics to find out about: physical description, habitat, hunting and eating, raising young, general behavior. Make materials available for research.

Direct Experience

Instruct students to work cooperatively to fill in the chart with key words and phrases about their animal. Once the information is gathered, have them explain their information to their group members as a way to practice for a one to two minute presentation to the whole class. Tell the students before beginning their practice exactly what you are expecting in their presentation. You may want to choose three or four criteria from the following. Did they: explain information accurately, stand with good posture (did not slouch or fidget), speak loudly so everyone could hear, make eye contact with the audience, remain poised (did not giggle). At the end of the practice session, have each group member share something positive about the other members' presentations.

Share Inspiration: Groups can make their presentations on the following day. Follow each presentation with "appreciations" by class members who share a positive comment about what they enjoyed, learned, or appreciated about the presentation (allow three to five appreciations per presentation). The teacher can either share a general appreciation for the whole group or give each individual group member a personal appreciation.

Extension: Students can practice the thinking skill of analysis by charting similarities and differences in the various animal species. A large master chart can be compiled in the front of the room after each group's presentation.

Spots

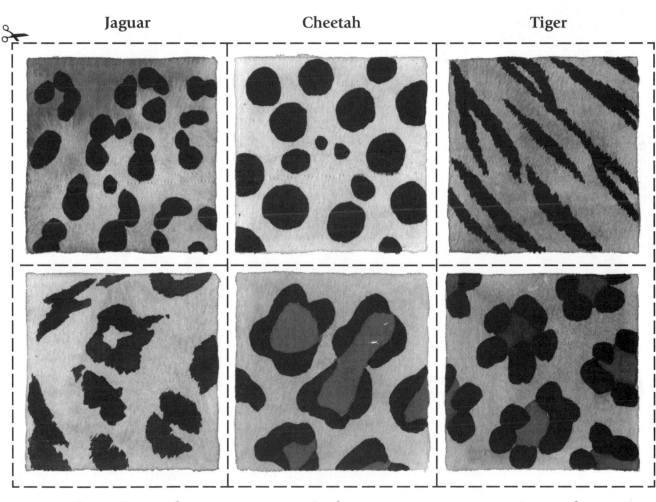

Jaguar	Cheetah	Tiger
Snow Leopard	Ocelot	Leopard

Copy Master for cut out

Kapok Tree

Friendship Is a Sheltering Tree

Objectives	• Acknowledge acts of friendship • Show appreciation of others
Tools of Maturity	• Feeling
Benchmarks	• Displays friendliness with others, displays empathy with others, contributes to the supportive climate in groups (Life Skills: Working with Others 4, Level IV); knows that all species ultimately depend on one another (Science 7, Level III)
Skills for Living	• Appreciation
Materials	• *The Great Kapok Tree* by Lynne Cherry; a deciduous tree branch that has many small branches and twigs but without its leaves (a "Friendship Tree"); container to hold the tree branch upright; paper cut into leaf shapes—several per student; paper clips—several per student • Time: Introduced in one class period, continued throughout the week.

Awaken Enthusiasm

Have students look at the picture of the kapok tree in *A Walk in the Rainforest*. Ask them what plants or animals they notice that depend on the kapok tree (vines grow on it, bromeliads grow on it, flowers grow next to it, birds perch on it, butterflies land on it). Ask them if they can think of any plants or animals that are not shown in the picture who might depend on it. Make a list.

Focus Attention

Read and Mind Map the information about the kapok tree. Add to the list any other ways that the kapok is helpful. Read aloud *The Great Kapok Tree*. As you read, add to the list any animals that depend on the tree. Point out that the kapok tree has giant buttress roots that give it support and keep it strong so it can then support others.

Write the following quote by Samuel Coleridge on the board: "Friendship is a sheltering tree." Ask students what they think it might mean. Explain that giving shelter can mean actually giving shelter like the kapok does, or it can mean being kind, helpful, or serviceful; it can also mean just being a good friend.

Direct Experience

Ask students to brainstorm the people in their lives who give them support. Pass out leaf shapes and have students write the name of a person and how that person helps them on the leaf shaped paper. For example, "The crossing guard helps me to get across the street when there is a lot of traffic." Remind them to think of a variety of times and situations throughout the day: in the cafeteria, on the playground, when working in small groups, riding on the bus, walking through the hallways. Have students sign their names on the back of the leaves and hang them on the branches of the "Friendship Tree" using a paper clip. Tell students that they can add a leaf to the tree each time they notice an act of kindness, helpfulness, or friendship during the next week. As the teacher, model noticing kind and helpful actions done by students, which will encourage others to participate in the process.

Share Inspiration

At the end of the week, read all of the leaves. Discuss with students the ways that they are connected to others. Just as the plants and animals of the rainforest depend on one another, human beings depend on each other, too. Have students write a thank you note to one person who has been a "sheltering tree" for them.

Mind Map

fuzz used by natives at rear of blowgun darts

fuzz used as stuffing in life jackets

blown in wind and carried by river

cotton-like seeds

only in flood season, unlike other trees that flower in dry season

flowers

Kapok Tree

grows in African and American rainforests

150 - 200 ft. tall

supported by giant buttress roots

Kapok Tree

Objectives	• Identify situations when inner strength is needed • Identify strategies that help students feel an inner strength
Tools of Maturity	• Will
Benchmarks	• Selects the most appropriate strategy or alternative for solving a problem (Life Skills: Thinking and Reasoning 5, Level III); knows strategies for resisting negative peer pressure, knows strategies to manage stress (Health 4, Levels II and III)
Skills for Living	• Self-reliance, introspection
Materials	• Fruit salad made from various tree fruits (such as apples, pears, peaches, or oranges), tree spices and condiments (such as cinnamon, coconut flakes, or vanilla extract), and tree nuts (such as almonds, walnuts, or pecans)—1 small paper cup per student; plastic spoons—1 per student; poster, picture, or drawing of a tree (as large as possible) posted in front of the classroom; paper and pencil—1 per group; optional: *Sharing the Joy of Nature* by Joseph Cornell • Time: Allow 90 minutes for this activity.

Awaken Enthusiasm

Food is an excellent way to grab students' attention. At the beginning of class serve each student a fruit salad with a spoon. Ask them to wait until everyone is served before beginning to eat. While they are eating, ask them what the ingredients of the fruit salad all have in common. There will be a variety of correct responses; the necessary response is that they all come from a tree.

Focus Attention

Read the following quote from J. Donald Walters: "Trees standing firm hold the secret of inner power. Give us when tested the strength to endure." Tell students that they will get to experience how that inner power feels by doing the "tree pose." Speak in a clear, calm, strong voice and demonstrate the movements as you give students the following directions: "Begin by standing very straight and tall. Keep your chin level to the floor and find a fixed spot on the wall directly opposite you. By keeping your gaze on that spot you will be better able to keep your balance as you go into the pose. Rest your weight on your left foot and imagine you are sending roots down into the floor from that foot. Slowly bring your right foot up and place it at a right angle to your ankle. If that is comfortable, bring it up to rest at your calf or your knee. You can even try resting your right foot on the top of your thigh. Keeping your balance, bring your arms up at your sides and over your head, putting the palms of your hands together above your head. Stand firm and feel strength, power, and energy flowing from your roots (the soles of your feet) up to your leaves (the tips of your fingers). Slowly bring your arms down to your sides (you can imagine that they are your branches spreading out around your trunk) and then bring your right foot to the floor. Rest on both feet for a moment and enjoy the feeling of the stretch; then repeat the pose sending roots down from your right foot and bringing your left foot up." It can be helpful to teach the movements first, answering questions and correcting body positions, and then begin again, talking the students through the movements in a calm and focused manner without stopping. Optional: Depending on the ability of your students, you can follow this activity with a tree visualization. Take them through one year in the life of a tree by describing what happens to the tree during each of the seasons. Include some hardships for the tree to endure such as a forest fire, a strong winter storm, an attack by a woodpecker or an insect, or kids carving with knives into its bark. Be sure to describe how the tree remains firm and strong. (An excellent tree imagery activity is described in *Sharing the Joy of Nature* by Joseph Cornell.)

Direct Experience

Ask students if any of them felt more calm, focused, or balanced after doing the movement. Tell them that trees symbolize for us the qualities of strength and centeredness; important qualities to have when faced with challenges in life. Divide the students into groups and have them brainstorm the situations in their lives when they need inner strength; for example, when pressured by peers to do something that they know is wrong, before taking a test, getting up in the morning, going home to an empty house, taking care of a younger brother or sister, after being yelled at or having their feelings hurt. After brainstorming a long list, have student groups circle the five most common challenges that they have to face. Next to each challenge have them write down one or more strategies they use to face the challenge; for example, counting to ten when they are angry, singing a song out loud when they are afraid, calling a friend on the phone when they are alone, practicing beforehand what they will say when a friend asks them to cheat, steal, or use drugs.

Share Inspiration

Have each group role play one of their situations in front of the whole class. Afterwards, post the lists of challenges and strategies on a poster of a tree in the front of the class. Remind students that everyone and everything on earth is constantly faced with challenges; having strategies of how to meet those challenges with inner strength and power will bring them greater happiness in life.

Leaf-cutter Ant

Torn Paper Mosaic

Objectives	• Create a mosaic of a rainforest picture • Review the rainforest plants and animals and their relationships
Tools of Maturity	• Feeling
Benchmarks	• Understands how species depend on one another and on the environment for survival (Science 7, Levels II and III); knows that all animals depend on plants; some animals eat plants for food while others eat animals that eat the plants (Science 8, Level II); applies media, techniques, and processes with sufficient skill, confidence, and sensitivity that one's intentions are carried out in artworks (The Arts: Visual Art I, Level IV)
Skills for Living	• Creativity
Materials	• Colored construction paper—several sheets per student; other types of colored specialty paper such as tissue paper, cellophane paper, glossy paper, etc.; white paper for the mosaic background—1 sheet per student; pictures of mosaics; shallow boxes—1 per color of paper

Awaken Enthusiasm

Ask students if they know the meaning of the word "mosaic." While showing a picture of or an actual mosaic, explain that it is a picture created by using small pieces of material, often glass or stone. In a mosaic all of the small parts relate to each other, creating a larger picture. One part is not complete without all of the others. Tell them that they are going to make a torn paper mosaic and, like the leaf cutter ant, they don't need any scissors. Pass one piece of construction paper to each student. Have students tear the paper into small pieces not bigger than 1/2 an inch square. When finished collect the paper pieces in shallow boxes, one color per box.

Focus Attention

Ask students to choose one of the pictures from *A Walk through the Rainforest* to use as a model for making a mosaic. To save time, students can simply draw names out of a hat. (If doing the extension portion of this activity, also have someone make a picture of the rainforest scene on the last two pages of the book to refer to trees and plants in a general way.)

Direct Experience

Give students white paper and have them sketch a simplified version of their picture. Next have them collect from the boxes the colored pieces of torn paper they need for their picture. Have additional paper on hand for those who may need to tear more pieces. Instruct students to arrange all of the pieces before gluing any of them in place. (Remind students to be careful as they walk around the room; bumping someone's desk can totally disrupt a picture until the pieces are glued down.) Tell students to go back and fill in any spaces with overlapping pieces of paper and to add details with smaller pieces of torn construction paper or specialty paper. Students may also want to use colored markers for making finishing touches.

Share Inspiration

Display the pictures around the room and look at them from a distance. Variation: Have students work cooperatively in small groups to create a picture together on a large piece of paper or poster board. Make sure the paper is large enough and the group is small enough for everyone to work on the picture at the same time.

Extension: Explain to the students that just like all the pieces of the mosaic work together, all of the plants and animals in the rainforest work together; they are interdependent and interconnected. Have students tape one end of a piece of string to the edge of their picture. They should attach the other end to the edge of a picture that in some way shows a connection with theirs; for example, the anteater to the ant, the frog to the bromeliad. Ask if some pictures have more connections than others (water, trees, and plants will probably have the most connections).

Mind Map

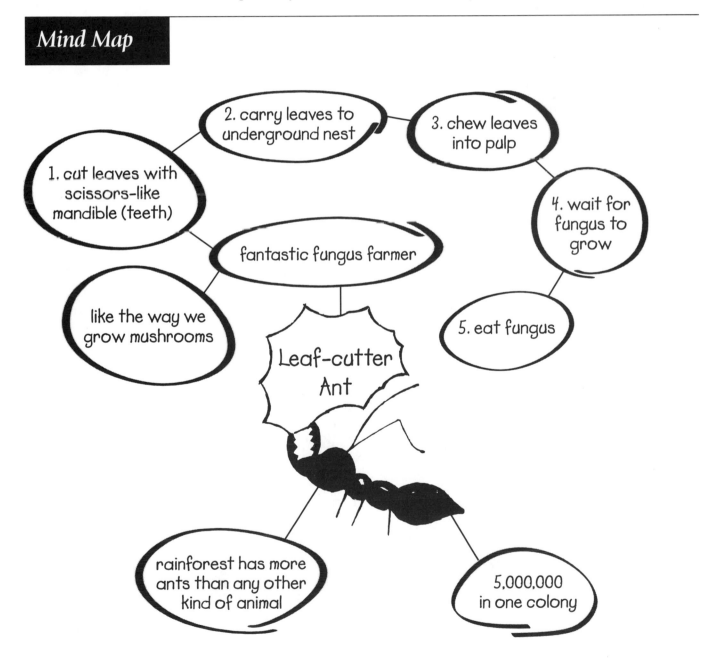

Leaf-cutter Ant

Step by Step

Objectives	• Set a goal and identify the steps necessary to achieve it • Steadily work towards accomplishing a goal
Tools of Maturity	• Will
Benchmarks	• Sets and manages goals (Life Skills: Self-Regulation 1, Level IV); practices perseverance (Life Skills: Self -Regulation 4, Level IV)
Skills for Living	• Perseverance
Materials	• Step-by-Step Chart (Copy Master, page 46)—1 per student • Time: Some time each day to record progress; additional time at the end of the month for celebration/certificate.

Awaken Enthusiasm

Ask if anyone in the class has eaten mushrooms. Do they know how they are grown? (Mushrooms are a fungus. They grow from a thread-like network called mycelium. Mycelium grows from spores, which are similar to seeds, that are dropped from the mushroom. Mycelium grow in damp, rich compost.)

Focus Attention

Tell students that leaf-cutter ants are called "fungus farmers" because they grow fungus to eat. They chew up leaves to create the right growing environment and it takes several steps before the ants' food is ready to eat. Randomly list the following steps on the board and ask the students to put them in the correct order. (1) Cut leaves from a rainforest plant. (2) Carry the leaves to their nest. (3) Chew the leaves and deposit them in their "garden." (4) Wait for the fungus to grow. (5) Harvest the fungus to eat. Check for accuracy by having the students read and Mind Map the leaf-cutter ant information from the book.

Direct Experience

Tell the class that achieving goals takes time. In order for the leaf-cutter ant to achieve its goal of getting food to eat, it goes through a step-by-step process. Each step takes time and energy. Ask the students to choose a personal goal they would like to accomplish within the next month. Explain that the best goals are very specific and measurable. For example, it could be an academic goal such as getting a 100% on a spelling test, a social goal such as planning and having a party, a physical goal such as being able to make eight out of ten free throws in basketball, or a financial goal such as saving money to buy a game. Explain that their goal can be broken down into little steps. The following are possible steps for earning a 100% spelling grade: (1) Write three lists of all the spelling words. (2) Post the lists on their mirror at home, inside their desk at school, and right next to their bed. (3) Write the words in a creative way each day: with ink, in pencil, in shaving cream, with bright colored markers, with little beans lined up to make the letters, etc. (4) Each day say the words aloud one at a time with their eyes closed and visualize the letters in their mind's eye. (5) Have someone test them on the words at least twice before the day of the spelling test. (6) Improve spelling test score by 10% each week. Let the leaf-cutter ants help the students reach their goals by using the Step-by-Step Chart. First, have students fill in their month-end goal inside of the ants' nest (see page 46). Next, have them write one activity they can do each day on one of the leaves. Allow time each day for students to record their progress on the chart by coloring in one of the leaves. (Twenty leaves equal one month of school days.) Encourage and remind students that accomplishing goals takes commitment. Making a little progress every day is a sure way to successfully accomplish what they want to do.

Share Inspiration

At the end of the month, honor the students' goals, efforts, and accomplishments with a certificate. Give additional recognition to those students who completed their goals, and encourage those who didn't finish to keep taking steps. During your celebration you may want to make and eat "ants on a log": spread celery with peanut butter (the log) and line raisins (the ants) along the top.

Certificate of Achievement

Well Done!

This certifies that

_____
(student name)

took _____ steps toward accomplishing the goal of

_____

*Signed*_____
(teacher's signature)

Date _____

Copy Master for cut out

Red-eyed Tree Frog

You Are What You Drink

Objectives	• Determine how much water the body needs each day • Learn characteristics of amphibians
Tools of Maturity	• Intellect, body
Benchmarks	• Knows how to maintain and promote personal health (Health 7, Level II); knows that living things can be sorted and classified into groups based on various properties (Science 4, Levels II- IV)
Skills for Living	• Vitality
Materials	• Beanbags, small balls, or small stuffed animals—1 per student group; paper and pencil—1 per student group; 8 ounce cups—1 per student; bathroom scale • Preparation: List of additional amphibian facts from "Focus Attention" section written on the board or overhead

Awaken Enthusiasm

Beginning class with a game engages student interest. Because frogs are known as great leapers, the game of "Leap Frog" is an excellent way to begin a class. An alternate game that requires less room and can easily be done inside is called "Over/Under Relay Race." Divide the class into even groups with seven to ten students per group. Instruct students to line up in single file within their group. Groups should position themselves next to each other with at least three feet between each of the lines. The first person in line is handed a beanbag (frog-shaped beanbags are available at many nature stores) and at a given signal passes the beanbag over his head to the person behind him. The next person in line passes the beanbag through (*under*) his legs to the person behind him. The third person passes the beanbag *over*; the forth *under*; etc. to the end of the line. When the beanbag comes to the last student, he runs to the front of the line and passes the beanbag *over* his head. To avoid collisions while running, have all students run on the right side of their line. Play continues until the original beginning student is at the front of the line again. Give enthusiastic applause and cheers for each group as they finish.

Focus Attention

Working in small groups, have students Mind Map the red-eyed tree frog from the information in *A Walk in the Rainforest*. Instruct students to include the following additional information about amphibians in their Mind Maps: amphibians live part of their lives in water and part on land ("amphibian" means double life); amphibians are cold-blooded, meaning they do not make their own body heat; they "breathe" through their skin (blood vessels in the skin take in oxygen from the damp ground or water); they "drink" through their skin (water is taken in through the skin and not through their mouths).

Direct Experience

Referring to the Mind Maps, point out that amphibians drink through their skin; therefore, living near water is essential for them. Explain that water is essential for human survival as well. Read the following list of interesting water facts. Tell students to give a "thumbs up" sign if they know the fact, a "thumbs down" sign if it is new information: water makes up about 75% of your body weight; the Earth has the same percentage of water as your body; water increases the amount of oxygen your blood can carry; you lose water every time you exhale (as water vapor); you lose two to three quarts of water a day. According to Dr. Paul Dennison, everyone needs one ounce of water per day for every three pounds of body weight. That's about one pint (two cups) for every 50 pounds. Have older students determine how much water they need mathematically. Divide their total body weight by three. That number equals the total number of ounces of water they need. Divide that number by eight which equals the number of glasses of water they should drink each day. (Since most students won't know their body weight, have a scale ready for the students to use.)

Share Inspiration

Have students drink an eight ounce glass of water.

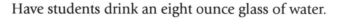

Mind Map

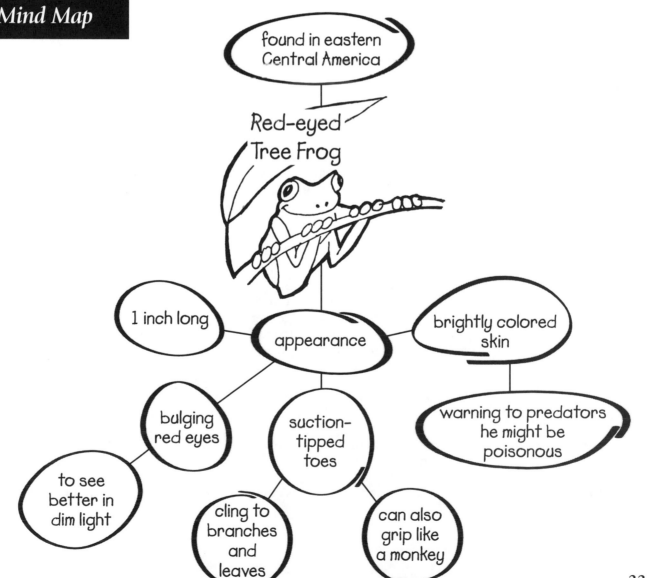

Sloth

Bad News to Good News

Objectives	• Practice looking at situations with a positive perspective
Tools of Maturity	• Feeling
Benchmarks	• Knows how to maintain mental and emotional health (Health 4, Level II and III); understands that there may be more than one valid way to interpret a set of findings (Life Skills: Thinking and Reasoning 4, Level III)
Skills for Living	• Positive attitude
Materials	• Paper and pencil—1 per student group

Awaken Enthusiasm

Ask the students if they think there are any "mistakes" in nature. Take responses.

Focus Attention

Mind Map the information in *A Walk in the Rainforest* about the sloth. Explain to the class that scientists originally thought that sloths were a mistake of nature because they move so slowly. Ask students to guess how long it took a mother sloth to "race" to the rescue of her baby. (A mother sloth was observed to take just over one hour to go 15 feet to rescue her baby. In the tree tops a sloth can go a little over 1 mph; on land 1/10 mph.) With further observation and understanding, scientists learned that in fact the sloth is perfectly adapted to its environment; by moving so slowly the sloth avoids detection by its predators, the harpy eagle and the jaguar. What was originally seen as a disadvantage for the sloth is actually an advantage.

Direct Experience

Explain to students that sometimes in their lives situations happen that appear to be a disadvantage, "bad news," but often by changing their attitude they can see how the situation is really an advantage, "good news." For example: bad news—they didn't get the part they wanted in the school play; good news—they got to be the stage manager. Bad news—their best friend is gone on vacation for a week; good news—they get to know the new kid on the block. Divide the class into small groups. Hand out a blank piece of paper to each group. Instruct the groups to fold their paper in half, making two columns, and to label the left column "Bad News" and the right column "Good News." Allow ten minutes for each group to list situations under "Bad News." When finished, each group passes their list to another group who has ten minutes to fill in the "Good News" column.

Share Inspiration

Have groups share their favorite situation with the rest of the class. Discuss how a positive attitude may not change the situation, but it can change how they feel about it. Practice positive thinking regularly in the classroom; it can become a habit that helps students through many difficult periods in their lives.

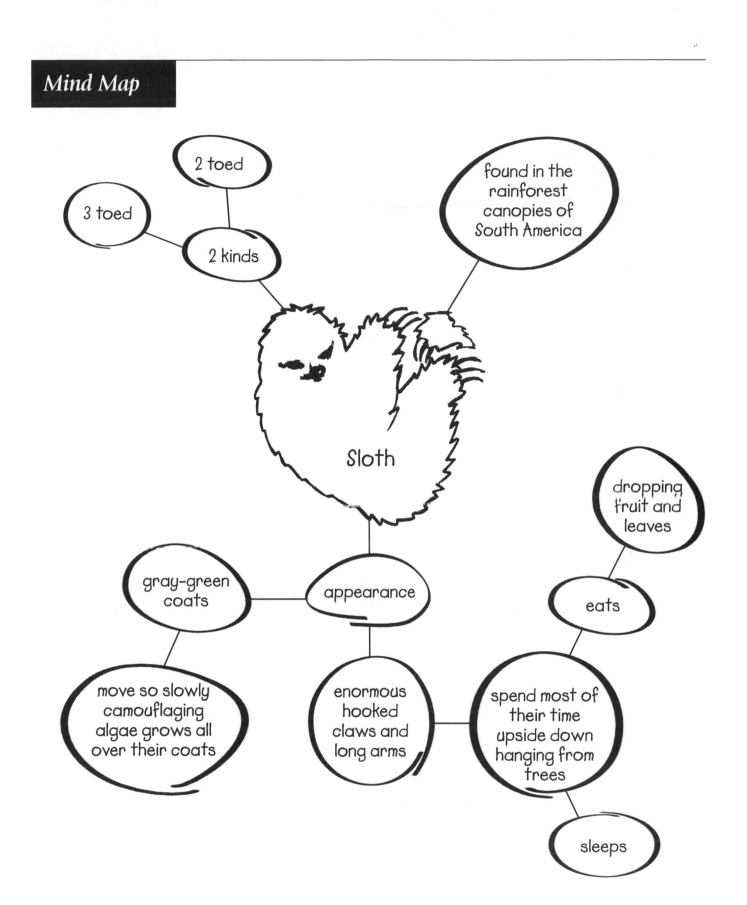

Sloth

Inside Algae

Objectives	• Label and color the structures of a plant cell
Tools of Maturity	• Intellect
Benchmarks	• Knows the general structure and function of cells in an organism (Science 6, Levels II and III)
Skills for Living	• Orderliness
Materials	• Plant Cell (Copy Master, page 37)—1 per student; either a transparency or large version of the plant cell to be used in the front of the room; sample of algae (available in dried form at many health food stores); microscope or hand lens; a prepared slide of a plant cell or, alternately, a thin slice of onion skin on a slide; colored pencils

Awaken Enthusiasm

Show the students the picture of the plant cell and ask them to guess what it is. After taking responses, tell them it is a picture of a single cell. A cell is the smallest structure of living matter that can function independently. All plants and animals are composed of one or more cells. Write the word "algae" on the board and ask students if they know what it means. (Algae is a one-celled plant.) If possible, show a sample of algae.

Focus Attention

Have students look at algae under a microscope. If a prepared slide is unavailable, a simple microscope or hand lens can be used to view the single cells in a piece of onion skin (a plant cell). Ask students what jobs they think a plant cell performs.

Direct Experience

Pass out copies of the Plant Cell Copy Master. Read aloud the names of the cell structures and the actual functions they perform. Tell students to color the plant cell. They can also label each structure with the correct name using the function that is listed below it as a clue.

Share Inspiration

Display the completed colored cells around the room.

Plant Cell

Cell Structures—Functions

cell wall—located outside of the cell membrane, gives strength to the cell
golgi bodies—secrete cell products and help make protein
cell membrane—allows nutrients to come into the cell and wastes to go out
endoplasmic reticulum (with ribosomes)—where protein for the cell is made
vacuole—sac filled with salt solution
nucleus—determines the nature of the cell and directs its activities
cytoplasm—liquid substance of the cell that holds other cell parts
chloroplast—contains chlorophyll, represents a "factory" for photosynthesis
mitochondria—converts sugar into energy for the cell

Color and Label

____
located outside of the cell membrane, gives strength to the cell

____
secrete cell products and help make protein

____
allows nutrients to come into the cell and wastes to go out

____
where protein for the cell is made

____
sac filled with salt solution

____
determines the nature of the cell and directs its activities

____
liquid substance of the cell that holds other cell parts

____
contains chlorophyll, represents a "factory" for photosynthesis

____
converts sugar into energy for the cell

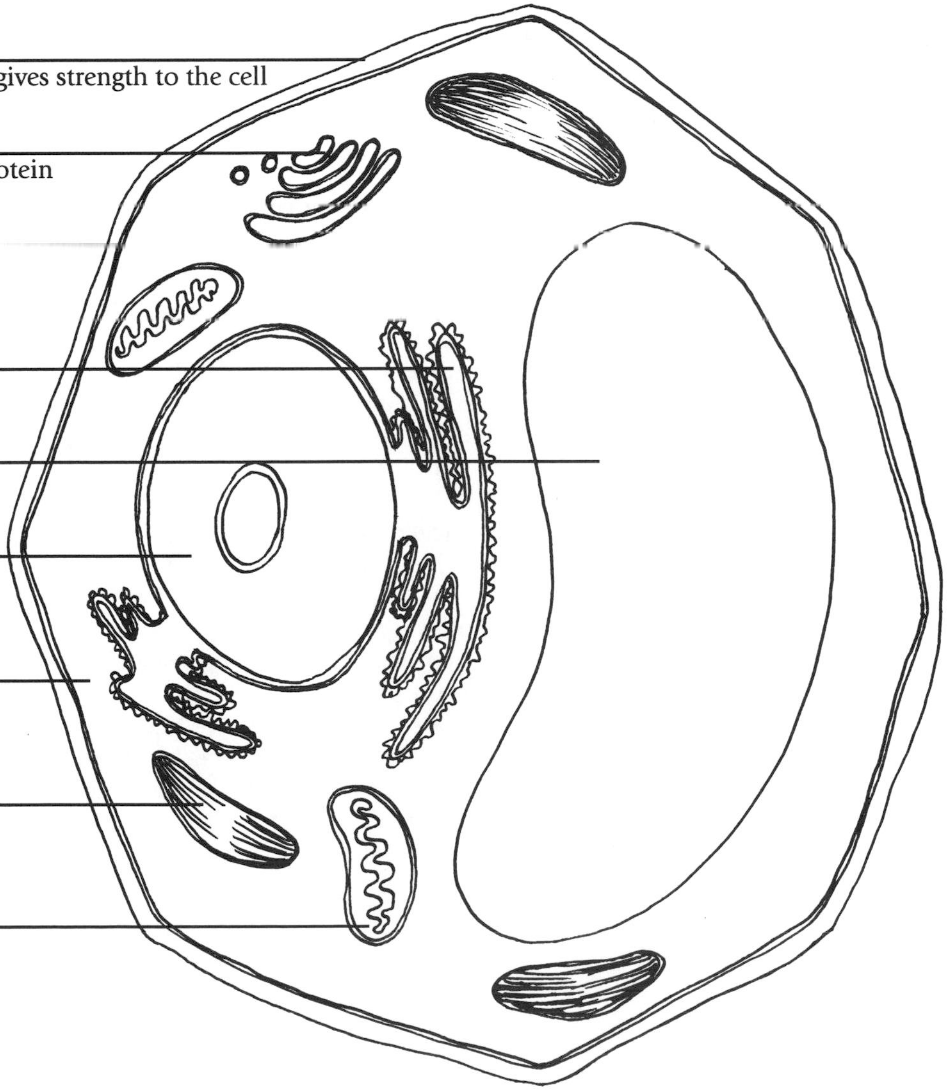

Copy Master

Vanilla Orchid

Epiphytes

Objectives	• Take care of a plant and observe its growth and changes
Tools of Maturity	• Feeling
Benchmarks	• Knows that plants require air, water, and light (Science 6, Level I); keeps a notebook that describes observations made (Life Skills: Thinking and Reasoning 4, Level I)
Skills for Living	• Dependability
Materials	• Variety of small house plants with care instructions—1 per student (ask a local nursery to donate them or to give them to you at the wholesale cost); science notebook or journal - 1 per student; optional: illustrated books on house plants
	• Time: Some time each week to update their journals, and after several weeks, additional time to share observations.

Awaken Enthusiasm

Explain to students that they are going to try to do a very simple task: standing up; but they cannot do it alone. They must have a partner. Have students pair off and sit down on the floor with their backs to each other. Instruct them to link arms and stand up without using their hands to touch the floor. (It is possible if they exert equal pressure on each other's backs while pushing upward at the same time.)

Focus Attention

Ask the students what helped to make standing up possible. What strategies did they use? Was it possible for only one person to stand up without the help of the other person? Could they depend on their partner to help? Explain to the class that in an ecosystem such as the rainforest, the plants and animals depend upon each other. Ask them if they know any examples of interdependency. Read aloud the information in *A Walk in the Rainforest* about the vanilla orchid; because the passage refers to the bromeliad and fern, read the passages about them as well. Discuss the term "epiphyte." (Epiphytes depend on the trees for their survival. All plants need light, water, and nutrients to grow. The trees give support to the plants so that they can grow closer to the sunlight, and the rainwater washes down nutrients from the debris in the trees that epiphytes need to exist).

Direct Experience

Show students the selection of house plants. Have them each choose a plant for which they would like to be responsible. Instruct students to carefully observe their plant and to draw a detailed picture of it in their science notebook or journal, including measurements of its height and size of its leaves. Have them read the care instructions for their plant and choose the best place in the room for their plant to grow. Encourage them to look through illustrated house plant books to learn more about their plant. Allow time each week for students to update their journals with new pictures,

38

measurements, and observations. They should be sure to date each entry. The plant can also become the main character in a creative writing assignment by having students tell a story from the plant's perspective.

Share Inspiration

Remind students that they are the only ones who will be taking care of their plant. Its growth and health depend on them. After several weeks, have students tell the rest of the class about the changes and growth they have observed.

Mind Map

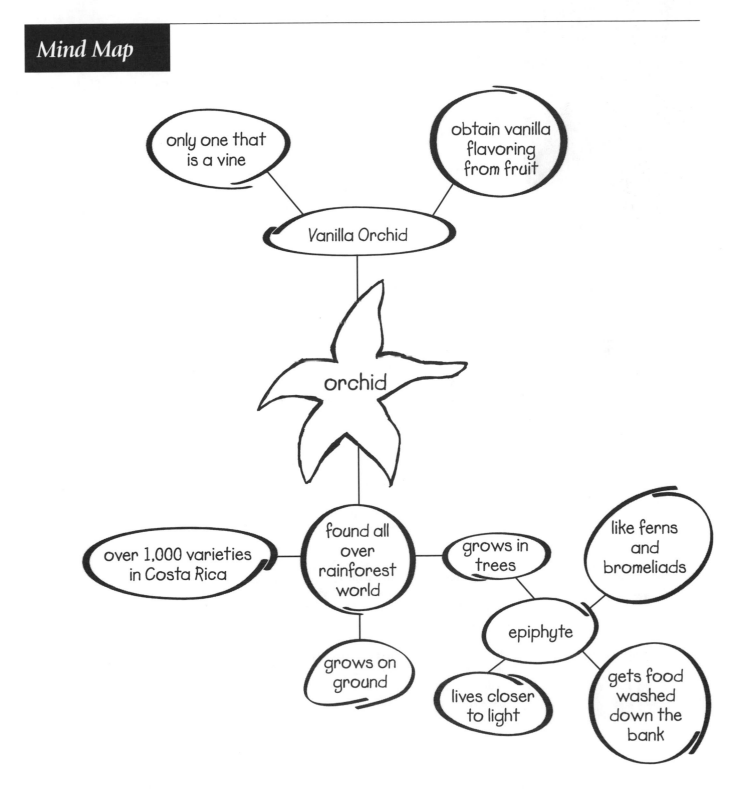

Vanilla Orchid

A Time for Every Purpose

Objectives	• Become more aware of appropriate behavior
Tools of Maturity	• Will
Benchmarks	• Displays effective interpersonal communication skills (Life Skill: Working with Others 4, Level IV)
Skills for Living	• Discrimination, self-control
Materials	• Behavior Situations (Copy Master, page 41); pictures of various orchids; seed catalog with pictures of various hybrid plants

Awaken Enthusiasm

Show the class pictures of different kinds of orchids. Explain that orchids are one of the most abundant and varied of all plant families. Over 25,000 species have been identified and tens of thousands of hybrids have been created. (A hybrid is a new plant that is created by breeding two different plants together.) There have been so many successful hybrids created because the orchid is flexible, easily changed, and very adaptable.

Focus Attention

Ask the class about any other plants that are adaptable. Showing pictures from a seed catalog can spark interest. For example blue corn, foot long green beans, and white raspberries are all unusual hybrids. Luther Burbank is a famous botanist who developed a special variety of potato. He knew plants so well that he even was able to create a cactus without any spines. (He was wanting to create a food source for animals living in the desert.) The basic nature of the cactus was the same, but it had been adapted. Explain to the class that there are times when it is important for all people to be flexible and adapt to their surroundings; different circumstances call for different behavior. There is a time to be loud and a time to be quiet. Ask students to give examples of such times; for example, watching a football game is a time when it is OK to be loud and listening to an orchestra concert is a time to be quiet.

Direct Experience

Divide the class into small groups of three to four students. Give each group a list of Behavior Situations. Ask them to brainstorm one or more times when the behavior would be appropriate.

Share Inspiration

Have student groups choose three or four responses to share with the rest of the class. A wise man once said, "Learn to behave." If students know how to behave in all situations, they will feel comfortable no matter where they are or what they are doing.

Extension: Rules of behavior are called manners or etiquette. By learning and practicing their manners, students will be welcome guests anywhere. Discuss etiquette for meals and have an "Etiquette Dinner." Serve many different courses and have students practice eating with the correct utensil, using their napkin correctly, and carrying on polite conversation.

Vanilla Orchid - Behavior Situations

Complete each phrase with one or more ideas.

A time to be...

loud

quiet

messy

neat

dressed up

dressed casually

silly

serious

A time to....

say "please"

say "thank you"

hurry

wait

cry

laugh

smile

frown

be alert

go to sleep

Copy Master

Vanilla Orchid

Spice of Life

Objectives	• Understand the origin of some common spices • Bake banana spice muffins
Tools of Maturity	• Body
Benchmarks	• Measures and mixes dry and liquid materials in prescribed amounts (Life Skills: Life Work 1, Level II)
Skills for Living	• Cooperation, practicality
Materials	• Vanilla beans, vanilla extract, cinnamon stick, ground cinnamon, nutmeg seeds, ground nutmeg, ginger root, ground ginger, whole cloves, ground cloves; ingredients and baking utensils for spice muffins (see recipe under Direct Experience); optional: an orchid flower • Time: Allow 90 minutes for making, baking, and eating the muffins

Awaken Enthusiasm

As students come into class, have a demonstration table set up with the spices and the orchid flower. Encourage them to look at and smell the various substances.

Focus Attention

Hold up the vanilla beans and ask the class what they are. After taking responses, have a few volunteers come up to the front of the class and smell the vanilla extract. Ask them what they think it is. Explain that the vanilla extract is the flavoring that comes from the vanilla bean. The beans are actually seeds that grow inside the fruit pod of the vanilla orchid, a rainforest flower. Tell the class that there are many common spices and flavorings, in addition to vanilla, that come from tropical plants. Show the students the cinnamon stick, ask what it is and what part of the plant they think it came from (the bark). Then show the ground cinnamon with which they are probably more familiar. Do the same for the nutmeg (a seed from a tropical tree), cloves (the dried flower bud from a tree), and ginger (although often called a root, is actually a rhizome—a fleshy, root-like underground plant stem that forms shoots above and roots below).

Direct Experience

Tell the class that they are going to use the vanilla and these spices to make a special treat: banana spice muffins! Divide the class into groups of seven which will allow each child to measure and add both a dry and a wet ingredient. Each group will work at a station that has the following utensils and ingredients for making 12 muffins:

Muffin Recipe

Utensils
2 large bowls, 1 for wet and 1 for dry ingredients
1 small bowl to mash bananas
1 fork to mash bananas
1 cup measure
1/2 cup measure
measuring spoons: 1 tsp., 1/2 tsp., 1/4 tsp., 1/8 tsp.
2 large mixing spoons, 1 for wet and 1 for dry ingredients
flour sifter
muffin tins lined with paper muffin cups

Dry Ingredients
2 cups unbleached white flour
1 tsp. baking powder
1/2 tsp. salt
1 tsp. ground cinnamon
1/2 tsp. ground nutmeg
1/8 tsp. ground cloves
1/4 tsp. ground ginger

Wet Ingredients
2 large eggs (2 students)
1/2 cup vegetable oil
1 cup brown sugar
1/2 tsp. vanilla extract
1-1/2 cups of mashed banana (about 3 bananas) (2 students)

Procedure
Preheat oven to 350 degrees.
(Begin with the dry ingredients so you won't have to wash the measuring utensils.)
Measure and sift together all of the dry ingredients.
Mix together all of the wet ingredients, adding the bananas last.
Stir the dry ingredients into the wet ingredients.
Spoon the batter into paper lined muffin tins.
Bake 20 - 25 minutes, until golden brown. A knife inserted into the center of a muffin should come out clean.

Before beginning, have all students wash their hands using soap and hot water. Demonstrate how to measure each ingredient before having the assigned student measure it for their group. While the muffins are baking, the students can clean up their work area and Mind Map the information on the vanilla orchid.

Share Inspiration

When the muffins are done, eat them as a class. Discuss how all the ingredients worked together to form something that tasted better than the individual ingredients all by themselves. Explain that, in the same way, when they cooperate with the other students in class it can create a classroom environment that is friendlier, "sweeter," and more fun than when they stay separate from each other. Share any extra muffins with the school office staff.

Alphabet Book

Objectives	• Select and research a topic of personal interest • Write and illustrate an alphabet book
Tools of Maturity	• Feelings, will, intellect
Benchmarks	• Effectively gathers and uses information for research purposes (Language Arts 4, Level II and III, all topics); sets and manages goals (Life Skills 1, Level IV)
Skills for Living	• Creativity
Materials	• Paper; research information; various art supplies; optional: spiral binding and plastic covers • Time: Can take up to six weeks

Awaken Enthusiasm

As a class, brainstorm a large list of topics that could be the subject of a children's alphabet book. Some topics chosen by students in other classes have been computers, mountains, rivers of the world, outer space, flowers, and U.S. presidents.

Focus Attention

Have each student choose a topic that has special personal interest. Tell students to write their topic across the top of their notebook paper and list the alphabet down the left margin. Next to each letter, have students list words related to their topic that begin with that letter. Students can help each other with creative suggestions at this point, but if they can't find at least one word for each letter, they should choose a different topic. Once they have a variety of words for each letter, have them choose one word for each letter that they can illustrate and also write about.

Direct Experience

Explain to the class that a book like *A Walk in the Rainforest* takes a very long time to make; so instead of writing about every letter, they should choose only a few letters to research and write detailed paragraphs for. (Every class is different, but researching and writing about nine words kept my sixth grade students focused during a six week unit.) Have students illustrate *all* 26 words for their topic. Setting weekly goals will help keep students from feeling overwhelmed and also teach them about time management. Additional pages to make include a cover, a title page, a dedication page, an "about the author" page, and an acknowledgment page. Books can be spiral bound with a plastic cover sheet for protection.

Share Inspiration

Celebrate the completed project by having the students share their books with another class. Students may want to put their books in the school library where they can be checked out and enjoyed by others.

Information Chart

	Name of Animal
Physical Description	
Habitat	
Hunting and Eating	
Raising Young	
General Behavior	

Copy Master for Jaguar, Special Spots

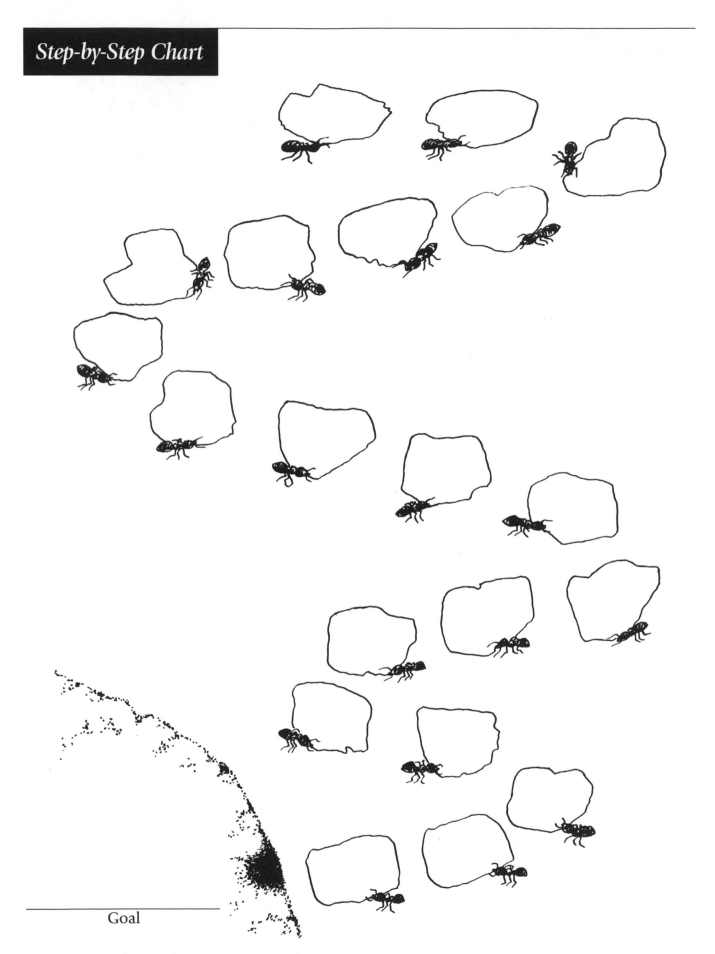

Goal

Copy Master for Leaf-cutter Ant, Step-by-Step

Sensitivity
showing understanding, caring, and kindness

Cooperation
getting along with others

Respect
showing regard for the worthiness of all creatures

Cheerfulness
having a positive attitude

Integrity
being truthful and honest

Concentration
being able to focus attention

Aspiration
striving for "personal best"

Self-Control
behaving appropriately

Vitality
being awake and ready

Perseverance
overcoming obstacles, determination

Servicefulness
helping others

Orderliness
being neat and organized

Dependability
being able to be counted on

Self-Reliance
taking responsibility for yourself

Creativity
approaching situations in fresh, new ways

Practicality
having common sense

Generosity
sharing with others

Introspection
being able to look within yourself

Problem-Solving
being solution-oriented

Curiosity
having a sense of wonder about the world

Appreciation
expressing gratitude

The above list represents some of the skills which Education for Life uses in its classrooms.

Body

go outside
do an aerobic activity
use props such as tennis balls, bean bags, balloons
wear a costume
perform a skit
play "Simon Says"
pantomime
eat a healthy snack
write letters in the air

Feelings

work with a partner
sing a song together
work in silence
make an art project
listen to music
share in a circle
hold hands
listen to a story
sing instructions
speak in accents

Will

perform challenges
(sitting still, turning over cards, writing words, etc.)
beat the clock in completing an activity
do circle rhythm clapping
play "Simon Says"
balance activities
(book on head, stand on one foot, etc.)
work in silence
follow the leader
give up something for one day
do something you've never done before

Intellect

read informational books
do mental math
practice skip counting
take a test
write down your thoughts
learn a new science concept
find locations on a map or globe
solve a problem
brainstorm

Smart Moves: Why Learning Is Not All In Your Head, by Carla Hannaford
Your Child's Growing Mind: A Guide to Learning from Birth to Adolescence, by Jane Healy, Ph.D.
Mapping Inner Space: Learning and Teaching Mind Mapping, by Nancy Margulies
Integrated Thematic Instruction: The Model, by Susan Kovalic
Super Teaching, by Eric Jensen
Training the Teacher as a Champion, by Joseph Hasenstab
Education for Life, by J. Donald Walters
Tribes: A Process for Social Development and Cooperative Learning, by Jeanne Gibbs
Megaskills: How Families Can Help Children to Succeed in School and Beyond, by Dorothy Rich
Self-Starter Kit for Independent Study, by E. Doherty and L. Evans
Nature Scope Tropical Rainforests, by The National Wildlife Federation
Brain Gym, by Paul and Gail Dennison
The Great Kapok Tree, by Lynne Cherry

Related Resources from Dawn Publications

Un Paseo Por El Bosque Lluvioso, Spanish version of *A Walk in the Rainforest*
Rainforest Animals Clue Game, by Joseph Cornell
XYZ the Ant Puppet
Sharing Nature with Children, by Joseph Cornell
Sharing the Joy of Nature, by Joseph Cornell
A Drop Around the World, by Barbara Shaw McKinney

DAWN Publications is dedicated to inspiring in children a sense of appreciation for all life on Earth. For a copy of our catalog, or for information about school visits by our authors and illustrators, please call 800-545-7475. Please also visit our web site at www.DawnPub.com, or e-mail us at DawnPub@oro.net.